French - Albanian

LEARNING FLASHCARDS

FOR BABIES TODDLERS

alligator

aligator

The alligator is having a party.

fourmi

milingonë

The ant is red.

ours

bear

The bear loves you.

abeille

bletë

The bee is saying hello.

oiseau

zog

The bird is flying.

papillon

flutur

The butterfly is pretty.

chameau

deve

The camel has a hump.

chat

mace

The cat is happy.

dinosaure

dinozaur

The dinosaur is laying eggs.

poulet

pulë

The chicken is dancing.

vache

lopë

The cow has a bell.

cerf

dre

The reindeer has a toy.

chien

qen

The dog has two floppy ears.

dauphin

delfin

The dolphin is swimming.

canard

rosë

The duck has a bow.

aigle

shqiponjë

The eagle is looking for food.

l'éléphant

elefant

The elephant is sitting.

poisson

peshk

The fish is a clownfish.

libellule

dragonfly

The dragonfly is blue.

renard

dhelpër

The fox has a red nose.

grenouille

bretkocë

The frog is smiling.

girafe

gjirafë

The giraffe has a long neck.

chèvre

dhi

The goat has a beard

ver de terre

rra

The worm is in the apple

poule

femër

The hen has chicks.

hippopotame

hipopotam

The hippo is big.

cheval

kalë

The horse is fast.

kangourou

kangur

The kangaroo has a baby.

chaton

kotele

The kitten is playing.

lion

luan

The lion has a mane.

homard

karavidhe

The lobster is red.

singe

majmun

The monkey has a tail.

poulpe

oktapod

The octopus has food.

hibou

buf

The owls have big eyes.

panda

panda

The panda wears a diaper.

porc

derr

The pig is fat and pink.

chiot

kone

The dog is brown.

lapin

lepur

The rabbit has a carrot.

rat

mi

The mouse is writing something.

crabe

gaforre

The crab has two pinchers.

requin

peshkaqen

The shark is scary.

mouton

dhen

The sheep are very fluffy.

escargot

kërmill

The snail is slow.

serpent

gjarpër

The snake has poison.

araignée

merimangë

The spider is purple.

écureuil

ketri

The squirrel has a nut.

tigre

tigër

The tiger has a red bow.

tortue

breshkë

The turtle has a shell.

loup

ujk

The wolf is smiling.

zèbre

zebër

The zebra is black and white.

dinde

turqi

The turkey has two legs.

coq

gjel

The rooster will crow.

perroquet

papagall

The parrot is colorful.

hérisson

iriq

The hedgehog has apples.

pomme

mollë

The apple has a leaf.

abricot

kajsi

The apricot is yellow.

avocat

avokado

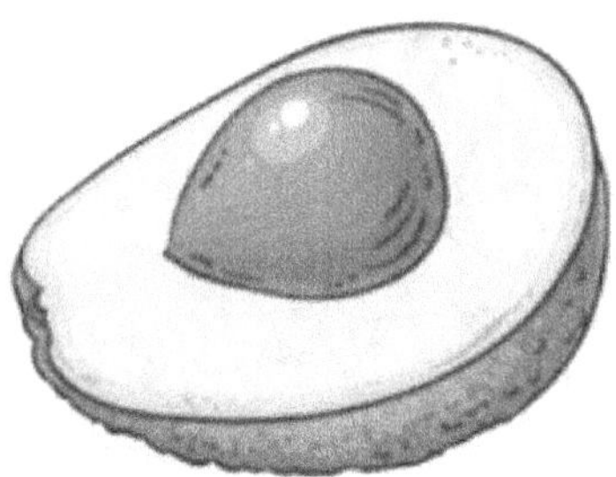

The avocado has a nut.

banane

banane

The banana is yellow.

la mûre

ferrë

There are a lot of blackberries.

cassis

blackcurrant

The blackcurrants are yummy.

myrtille

boronicë

The blueberries are sweet.

cerise

qershi

The cherries have a stem.

noix de coco

i kokosit

The coconuts have juice.

figues

fiq

The fig has seeds.

grain de raisin

hardhi

The grapes are purple.

pamplemousse

grejpfrut

The grapefruits are sour.

kiwi

kivi

The kiwi is fresh.

citron

limon

The lemons are yellow.

citron vert

gëlqere

We have lots of lime.

litchi

lychee

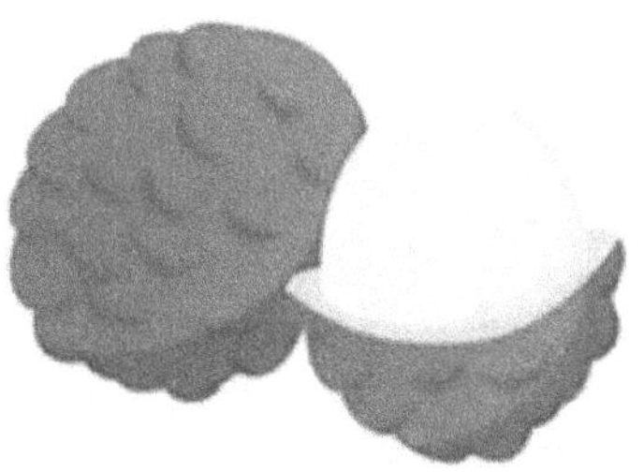

I like to eat lychee.

mandarine

mandarinë portokall

Oranges are refreshing.

mangue

mango

Mango is my favorite fruit.

orange

portokall

Mandarins are like oranges.

papaye

papaja

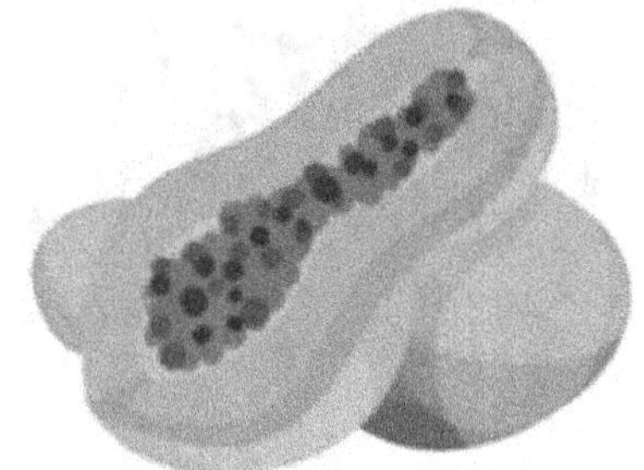

Papayas have lots of seeds.

pêche

pjeshkë

Peaches are juicy.

poire

dardhë

Pears have a strange figure.

ananas

ananasi

The pineapple has a thumbs up.

prune

llokum

Plums are healthy for you.

grenade

shegë

Pomegranates are all red.

framboise

mjedër

The raspberry is shiny.

fraise

luleshtrydhe

The strawberry has leaves on top.

pastèque

shalqi

The watermelon is big.

mandarine

mandarinë

The tangerine looks like an orange.

tarte

byrek

I like to eat apple pie.

gâteau

tortë

That cake is huge.

bonbons

karamele

Candy is not good for your teeth.

biscuit

biskotë

Cookies are easy to make.

donut

petull

I like strawberry donuts.

crème glacée

akullore

The ice cream is melting.

muffin

kifle

The muffin has a cute wrapper.

pudding

buding

We eat pudding on Christmas.

classeur

kordon

I keep pictures in my binder.

livre

libër

I like to eat books.

sac à dos

çantë shpine

The backpack has lots of stuff.

les ciseaux

gërshërë

I have scissors in my bag.

épingles

këmbët

Pins can hold stuff up.

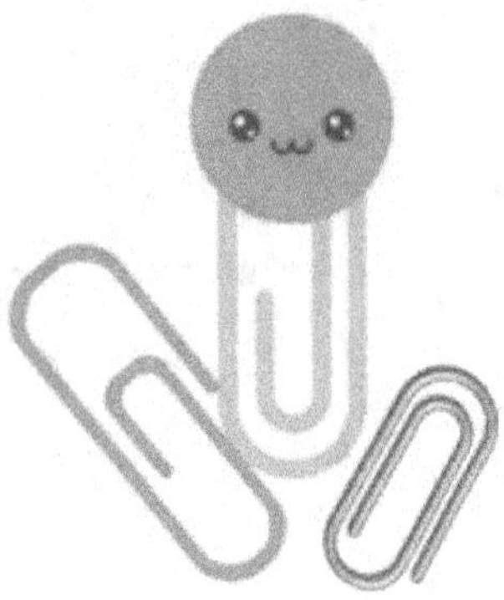

agrafe

kapëse

Clips can hold up paper.

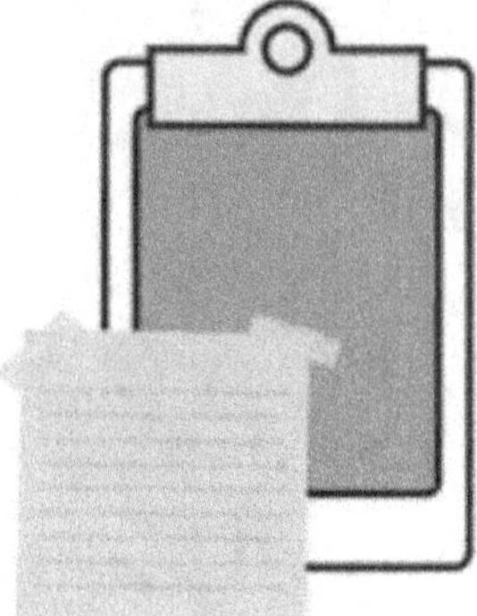

papier

letër

I have lots of paper.

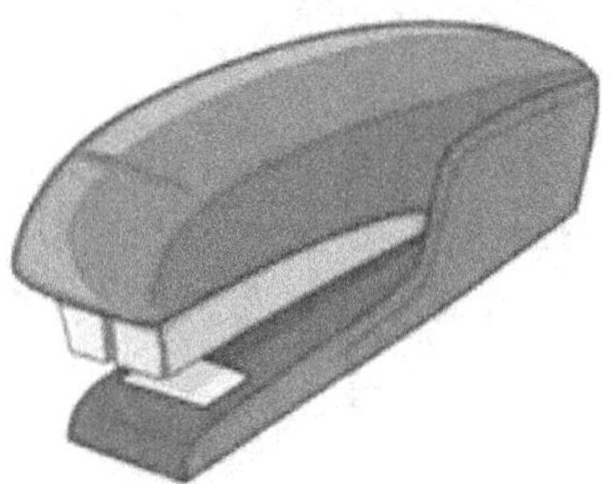

agrafeuse

seleksionues fijesh

My stapler is shiny and red.

calculatrice

kalkulatriçe

My calculator has buttons.

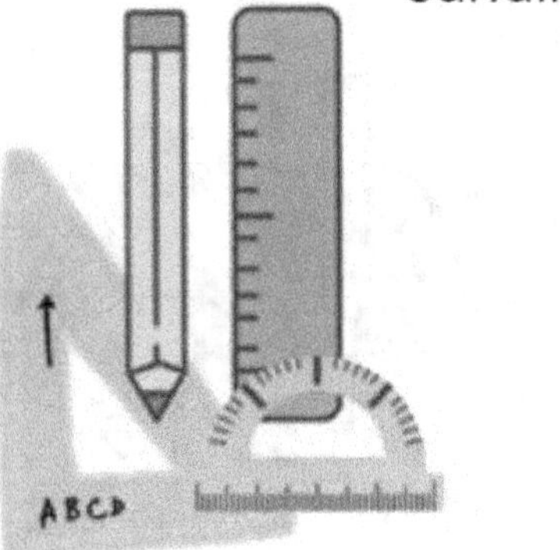

règle

sundimtar

I have lots of rulers.

la colle

zam

The glue is sticky.

bibliothèque

raft librash

My bookcase has lots of things.

calendrier

kalendar

I have a calendar on my table.

chaise

karrige

My chair is fancy.

l'horloge

orë

The clock says that it's 3 o'clock.

ordinateur

kompjuter

I do things on my computer.

bureaux

tavolina

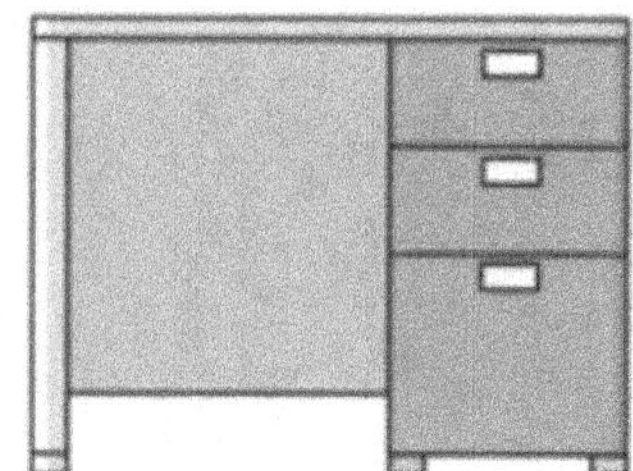

I put lots of things on my desk.

dictionnaire

fjalor

The dictionary has lots of words.

la gomme

gomë

Erasers are used with pencils.

carte

hartë

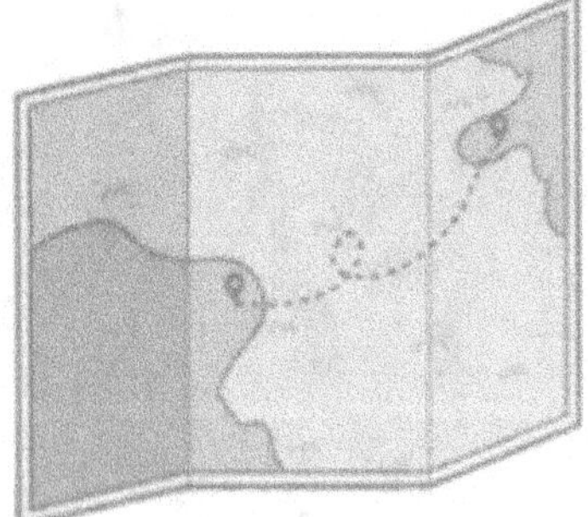

The map shows you different places.

carnet

fletore shënimesh

I use notebooks at school.

stylo

stilolaps

My pen is very pretty.

crayon

laps

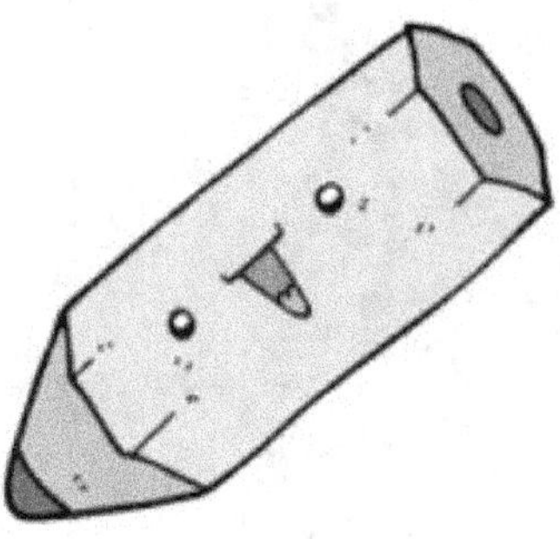

My friend gave me a pencil.

ceinture

rrip

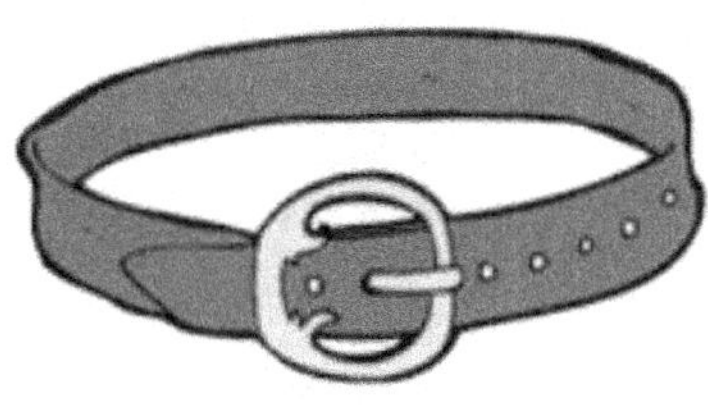

I have a belt on my pants.

bottes

çizme

I have big brown boots.

chapeau

kapelë

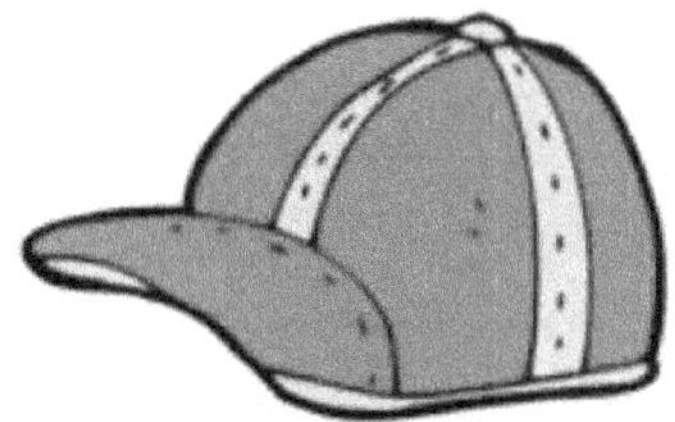

My mom bought me a new cap.

manteau

shtresë

She has a long yellow coat.

robes

dresses

My dress has a bow.

gants

dorashka

I got new gloves.

chapeau

kapelë

That hat is for a wicked witch.

veste

xhaketë

The jacket is cozy.

jeans

xhinse

My jeans are long.

pyjamas

pizhamë

I sleep in my pajamas.

un pantalon

pantallona

The bear is wearing pants.

imperméable

mushama

We wear our raincoats when it is raining.

écharpe

shall

The baby has a scarf around his neck.

chemise

këmishë

I like this shirt the best.

des chaussures

këpucët

I have red and blue shoes.

jupe

pantallona të gjera

My skirt has lots of buttons.

pantalon

pantallona të gjera

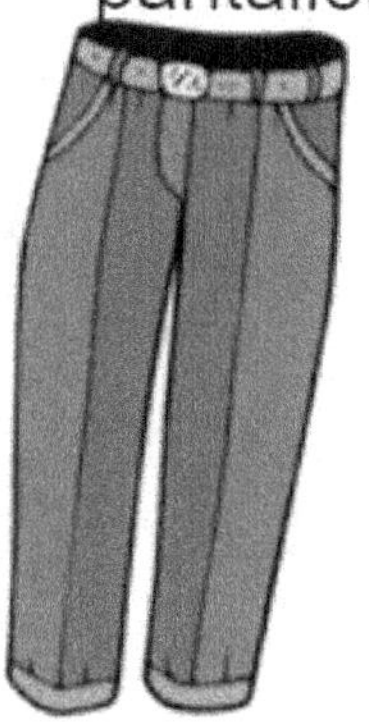

My dad wears slacks.

chaussons

pantofla

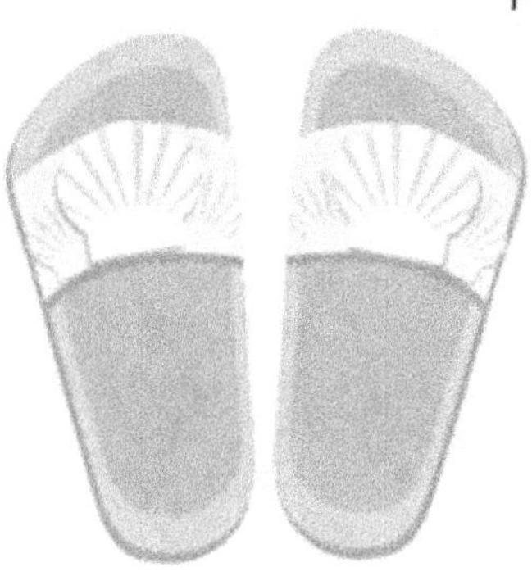

I have seashells on my sandals.

chaussettes

çorape

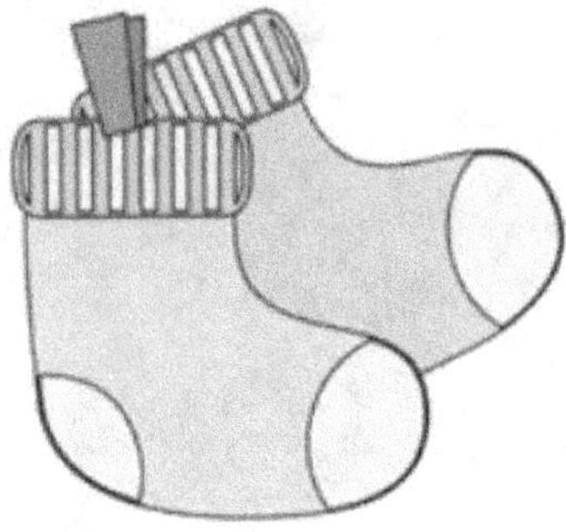

My baby sister wears socks.

costume

kostum

My brother is wearing a suit.

chandail

triko

I am wearing a sweater for winter.

cravate

kravatë

My dad wears a tie to meetings.

pantalon

pantallona

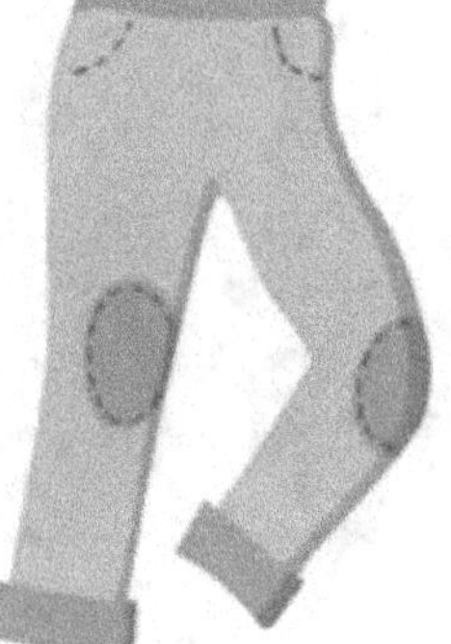

The trousers look like jeans.

slip

brekë

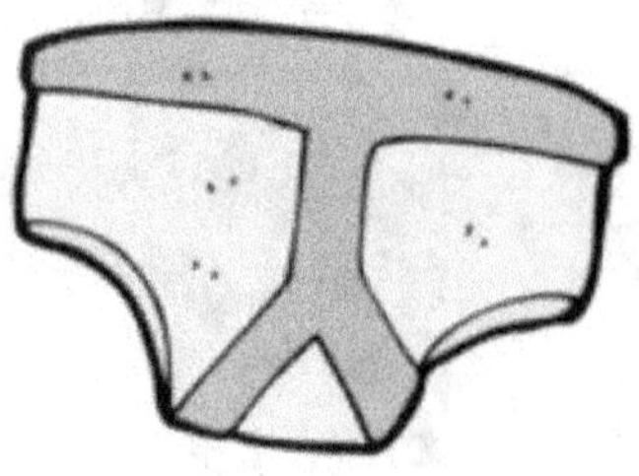

I always wear my underwear.

maillot de corps

fanellërë

My undershirt has a star.

une

një

Number one and the bee are friends.

deux

dy

The cat and the mouse both love two.

trois

tre

The bear gives number three a present.

quatre

katër

Number four is a home for the cat.

cinq

pesë

Number five hatches an egg.

six

gjashtë

Number six is going to eat a carrot.

sept

shtatë

Number seven is playing with the tiger.

huit

tetë

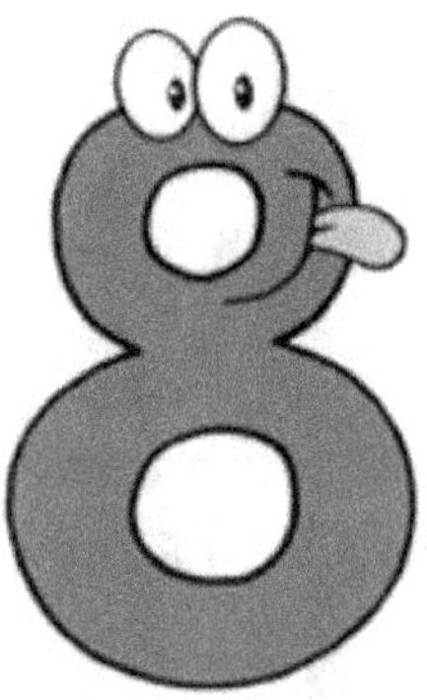

Number eight is funny.

neuf

nëntë

Number nine meets the parrot.

dix

dhjetë

Number ten is smiling.

onze

njëmbëdhjetë

Number eleven has big eyes.

douze

dymbëdhjetë

Number twelve is number one and two.

treize

trembëdhjetë

Number thirteen is excited.

quatorze

katërmbëdhjetë

The number fourteen is vast.

quinze

pesëmbëdhjetë

The number fifteen is green.

seize

gjashtëmbëdhjetë

Sixteen is my lucky number.

dix-sept

shtatëmbëdhjetë

Number seventeen look alike.

dix-huit

tetëmbëdhjetë

Number eighteen will go to the circus.

dix-neuf

nëntëmbëdhjetë

I am nineteen now!

vingt

njëzet

Number twenty has a zero.

fourmi

milingonë

The ant has lots of legs.

cloche

zile

The bell will ring.

vache

lopë

The cow has a bow.

poupée

kukull

She has a cute bear doll.

oeuf

vezë

The chick has hatched out of the egg.

poisson

peshk

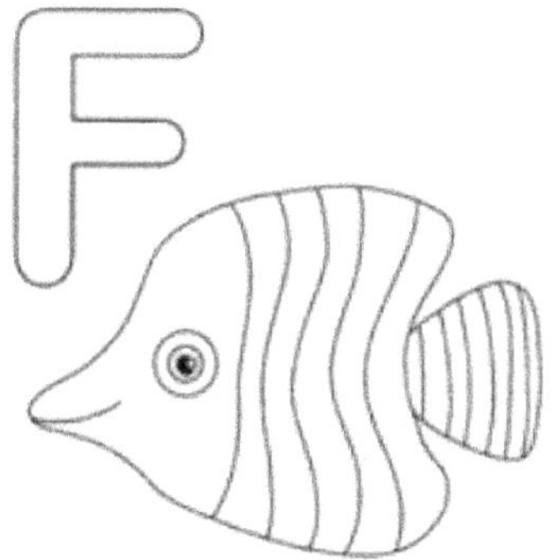

The fish is swimming in the water.

chèvre

dhi

The goat is sitting on the grass.

chapeau

kapelë

He is wearing a hat.

crème glacée

akullore

I like to eat ice cream.

confiture

bllokim

The kitten is sitting on the jam jar.

chaton

kotele

The cat is sleeping on the floor.

lion

luan

The lion is waiting for the tiger.

rat

mi

The mouse has lots of presents.

nez

hundë

The reindeer has a red nose.

hibou

buf

The owl is sleeping.

porc

P

derr

The pig will eat cupcakes.

reine

Q

mbretëreshë

The queen has a big crown.

lapin

R

lepur

The rabbit is jumping up and down.

mouton

S

dhen

The sheep have fluffy wool.

tortue

T

breshkë

The turtle has a shell.

parapluie

U

ombrellë

The mouse is holding an umbrella.

van

furgon

The van is driving along the road.

pastèque

shalqi

The watermelon has lots of seeds.

xylophone

ksilofon

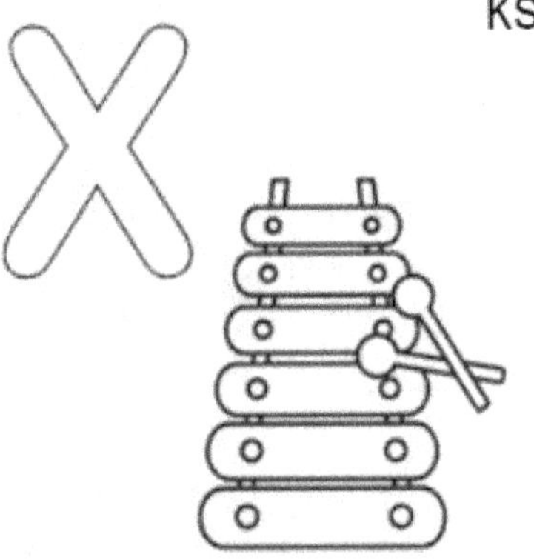

We are going to play the xylophone.

yaourt

kos

We opened the yogurt can.

zèbre

zebër

The zebra is surprised.

rose

rozë

color the word and the picture in pink

Most of my clothes are pink.

marron

bojë kafe

color the word and
the picture in pink

My chocolate is brown.

gris

gri

color the word and
the picture in pink

I don't like the color gray.

vert

e gjelbër

color the word and
the picture in pink

The vegetables are green.

jaune

e verdhe

color the word and
the picture in pink

Bananas are yellow.

blanc

e bardhë

color the word and
the picture in pink

The paper that I write on is white.

rouge

i kuq

color the word and
the picture in pink

Apples are red.

bleu

blu

color the word and the picture in pink

The night sky is blue.

percer

stërvitje

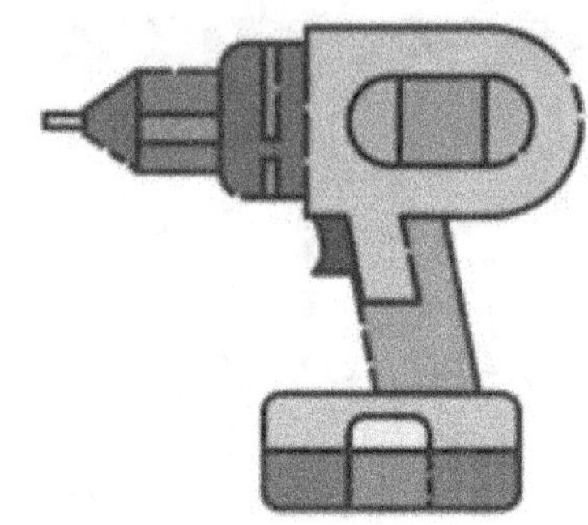

The drill will help us fix this.

marteau

çekiç

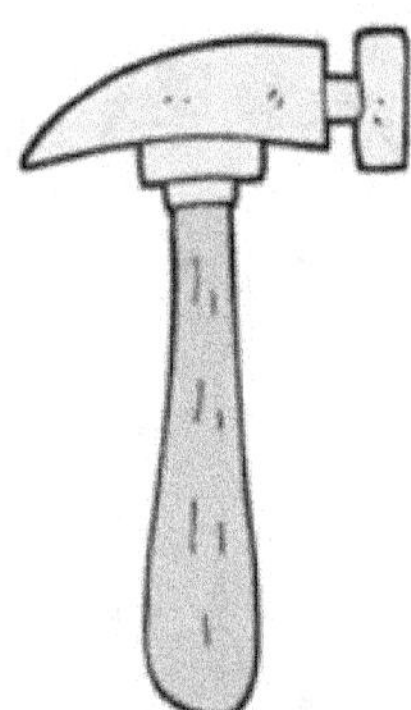

The hammer is going to nail the picture.

couteau

thikë

The knife is sharp.

pinces

pincë

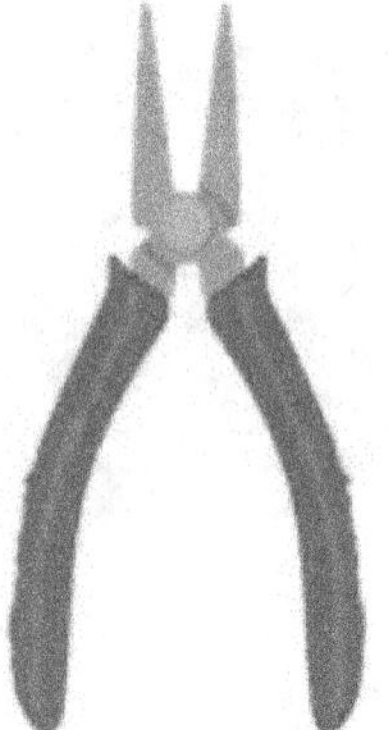

The plier is used for many things.

vu

sharrë

The saw can chop wood.

les ciseaux

gërshërë

I use scissors to cut paper.

tournevis

kaçavidë

The screwdriver can screw in the knots.

clé

pikëllim

The wrench can help unscrew the knots.

avion

aeroplan

The airplane is going to leave now.

vélo

biçikletë

The bicycle is beautiful.

bateau

varkë

The boat is floating on the water.

autobus

autobus

The bus is going to school.

voiture

makinë

The car is green.

hélicoptère

helikopter

The helicopter is looking for something.

cheval

kalë

You can ride the horse.

jet

reaktiv

The jet is high-speed.

moto

motoçikletë

The motorcycle is on the road.

navire

anije

The ship is on the water.

métro

metro

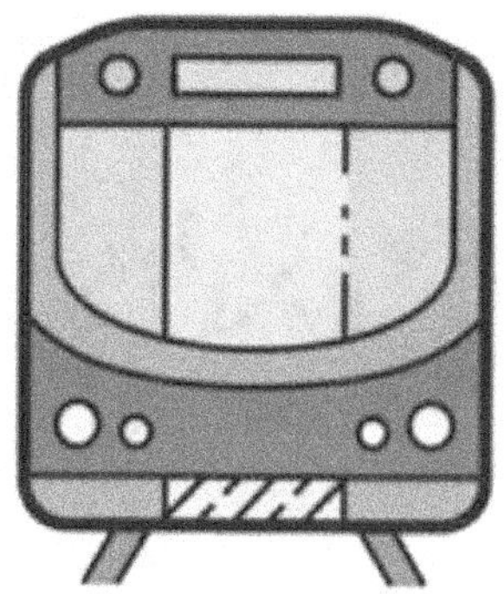

My mom goes on the subway to work.

taxi

taksi

The taxi has someone inside.

train

tren

The train is going slowly.

un camion

kamion

The truck has stuff in it.

asperges

shparg

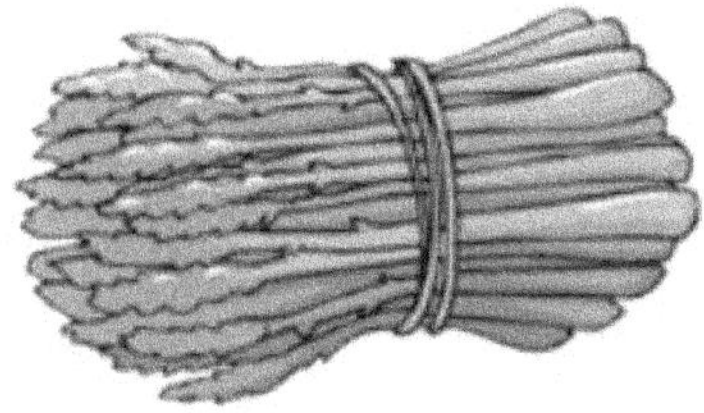

The asparagus is in a bundle.

des haricots

bathë

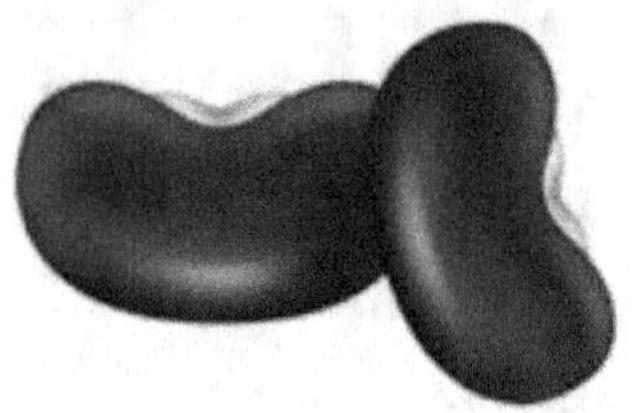

The beans are smooth.

brocoli

brokoli

The broccoli is dancing.

chou

lakër

Bunnies like to eat cabbage.

carotte

karotë

The carrots are very long.

céleri

selino

The celery has lots of leaves.

blé

misër

Corn soup is delicious.

concombre

kastravec

The cucumbers are cut into pieces.

aubergine

patëllxhan

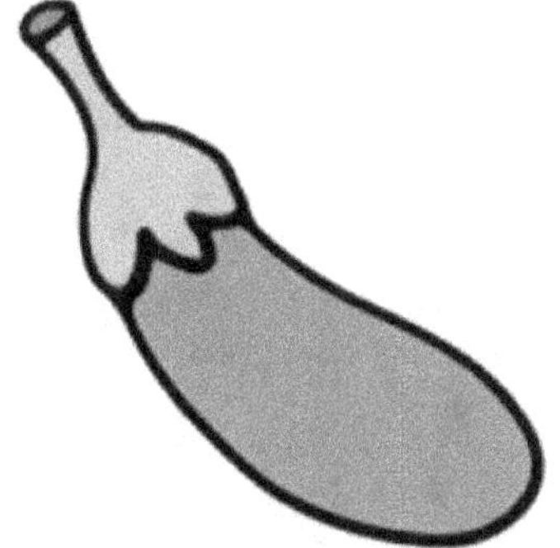

The eggplant is purple.

poivre vert

piper jeshil

The green pepper is juicy.

salade

marule

The lettuce is all green.

oignon

qepë

The onions make my eyes water.

pois

bizele

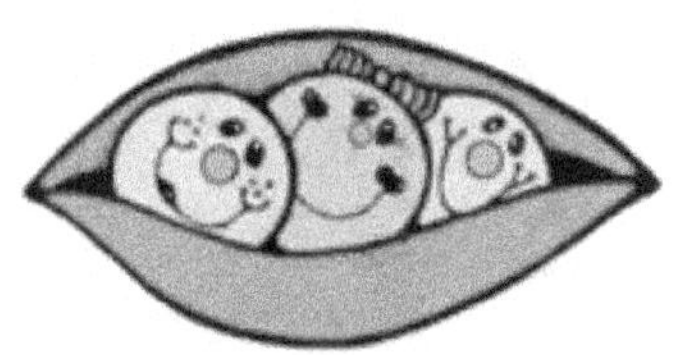

The peas are all in a pod.

patate

patate

The potato is very shiny.

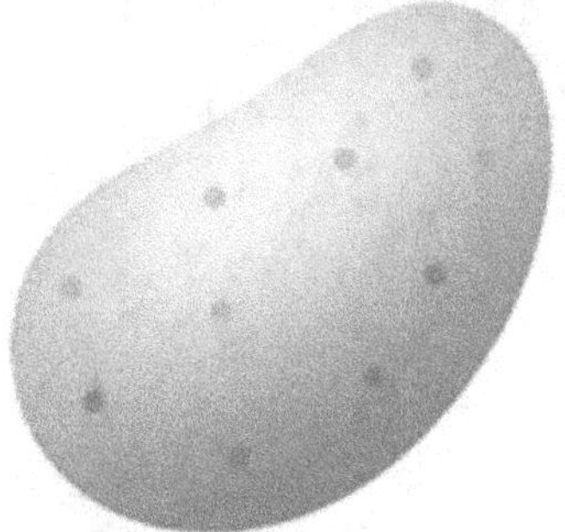

citrouille

kungull

The pumpkin is for Halloween.

un radis

rrepkë

The radish is a type of vegetable.

épinard

spinaq

The spinach is good with cheese.

patate douce

patate e embel

The sweet potato is quite sweet.

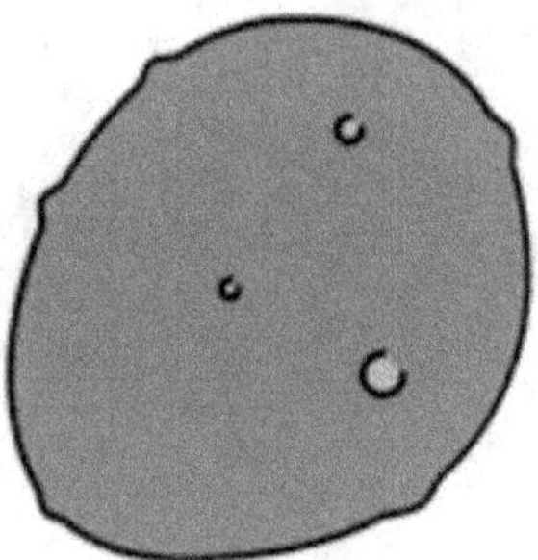

tomate

domate

I don't like to eat tomatoes.

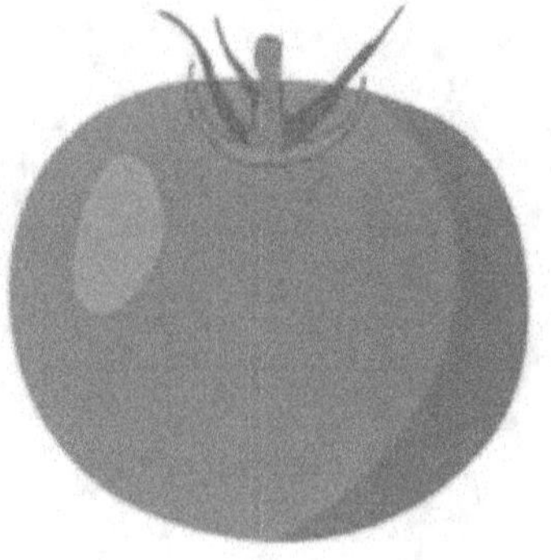

navet

rrepë

My mom bought some turnips.

nuageux

i vrenjtur

The weather is cloudy today.

du froid

të ftohtë

I like cold weather.

cool

i ftohtë

The temperature is cold today.

brumeux

i errët

The fog is so strong I can't see the city.

chaud

nxehtë

The fire is burning hot.

humide

i lagësht

It's so humid and wet today.

pluvieux

me shi

It's raining very hard.

neigeux

me dëborë

Welcome to snow land!

orageux

i stuhishëm

I hate the stormy weather.

ensoleillé

me diell

The sun is shining!

chaud

i ngrohtë

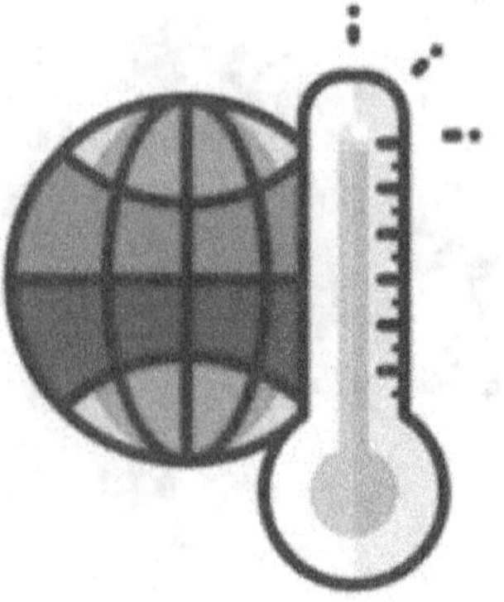

The whole world is warm today!

venteux

me erë

The leaves are blowing away since it's so windy!

tante

hallë

My aunt is very nice to me.

frère

vëlla

My brother is very fun to play with.

cousin

kushëri

I love going to the playground with my cousin.

fille

bijë

I like to read books with my daughter.

père

baba

My father is playing with me.

petite fille

mbesë

My granddaughter has blond hair.

grand-mère

gjyshe

My grandmother is very old and has glasses.

petit fils

nip

My grandson and I are very excited today!

mère

nënë

My mother likes to pick me up.

neveu

nip

My father's nephew is my cousin.

nièce

mbesë

My niece is very good at playing ball.

sœur

motër

My sister is so pretty!

fils

bir

My son likes to play with toy cars.

belle fille

thjeshtër

My stepdaughter likes the color orange.

belle-mère

njerkë

My stepmother is pretty.

beau-fils

thjeshtër

This is my stepson, Greg.

oncle

dajë

My uncle tells lots of funny jokes.

bol

tas

The bowl has nothing inside.

tasse

kupë

My mom drinks her coffee out of a cup.

plat

pjatë

That dish has a bone inside.

fourchette

pirun

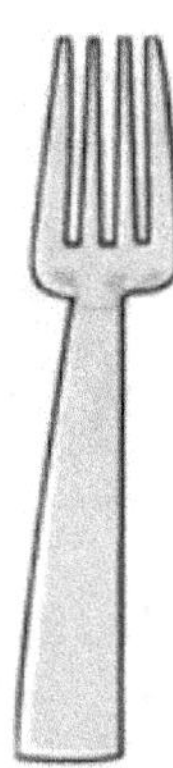

We have more spoons than forks.

verre

gotë

I have a glass of water on my desk.

couteau

thikë

I have a knife in my kitchen.

agresser

turi

This mug of coffee is for my dad.

serviette de table

pecetë

You can use the napkins to clean your hands.

poivre

piper

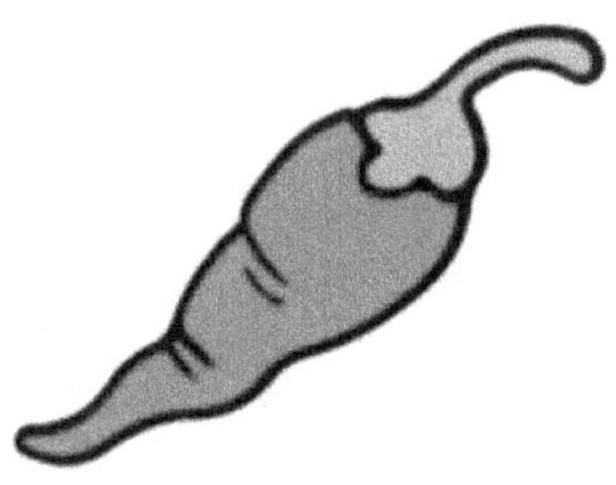

The pepper is very spicy.

lanceur

shtambë

Pour yourself some lemonade from the pitcher.

assiette

pjatë

Can you help me wash the plates?

salade

sallatë

The salad is very healthy for you.

sel

kripë

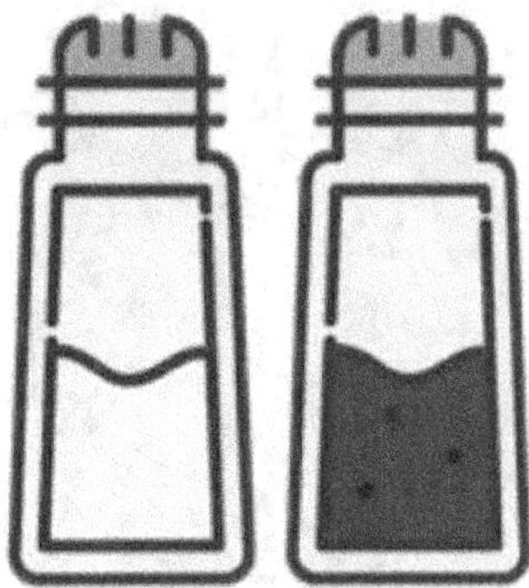

The salt tastes good with a few pinches of pepper.

soucoupe

pjatëz

The plate is for my cup.

cuillère

lugë

I use a spoon to eat my rice.

sucre

sheqer

The pack of sugar is very heavy.

dimanche

e diel

Sunday

Sunday is the day to go to Church!

lundi

e hënë

Monday

Monday is the day to start school.

mardi

e marté

Tuesday

We will go to the shops on Tuesday.

mercredi

e mërkurë

Wednesday

Wednesday is hard to spell!

jeudi

e enjte

Thursday

Thursday is the fourth day of the week!

vendredi

e premte

Friday

My birthday is on Friday!

samedi

e shtunë

Saturday

Saturday is the weekend!

cuire

piqem

The chef will bake a cake.

ébullition

vlim

I will boil the eggs.

griller

përvëlohem

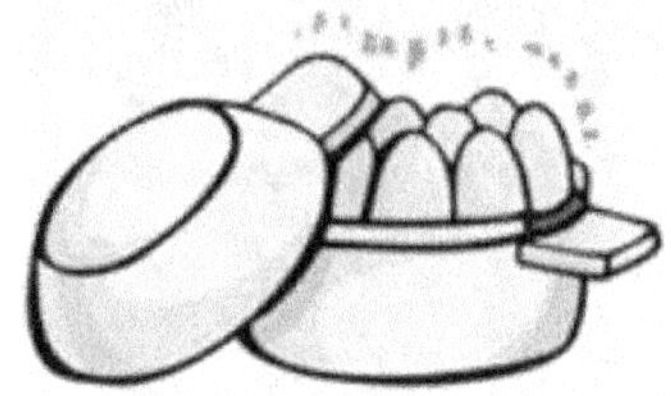

Broil is very yummy.

ouvre-boîte

hapës kanaçeje

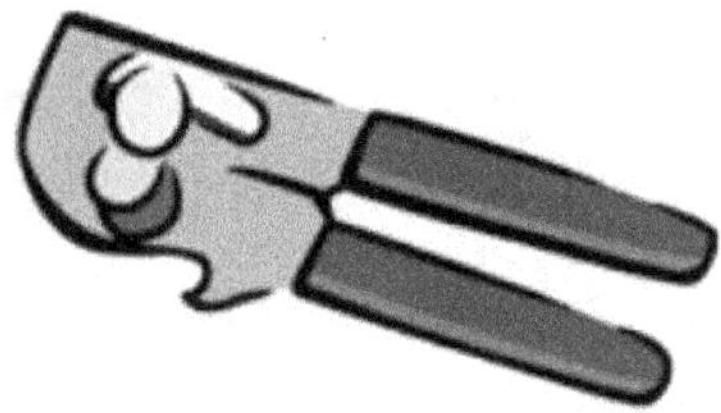

That can opener is used for opening cans.

frire

të skuqura

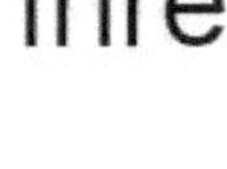

The pan can fry lots of things.

gril

vuaj

We have a grill in our backyard.

tasse à mesurer

filxhan matës

My mom uses the measuring cup for baking.

cuillère à mesurer

lugë matëse

I use a measuring spoon to eat my dessert.

four micro onde

mikrovalë

The microwave is used to heat food.

bol à mélanger

tas për përzierje

She is using the mixing bowl to mix things.

serviettes en papier

peshqir letre

Dry your hands with paper towels.

poché aux œufs

krushqia e vezëve

The poach is put on noodles.

porte pot

mbajtës tenxhere

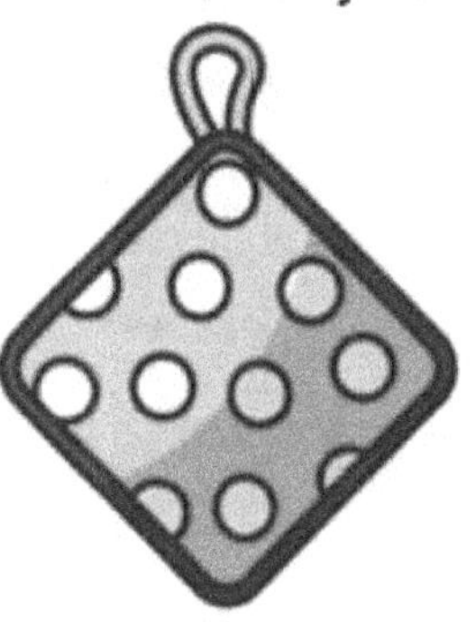

The potholder is soft.

rôti

rosto

The chef made roast chicken.

rouleau à pâtisserie

okllai

He is holding a rolling pin.

brouiller

përleshje

My mom is making scrambled
eggs for breakfast.

mijoter

zierje

The simmer is rice today.

couteau

thikë

The knife is sharp.

cuillère

lugë

I eat my food with a spoon and
fork.

spatule

shpatull

The spatula will help us flip the steak over.

vapeur

avull

The steam is coming from the pot.

passoire

sitë

The strainer is used to strain stuff.

minuteur

kohëmatës

I set my timer for 12:00.

fourchette

pirun

I have lots of metallic forks.

grille-pain

ai që thotë dolli

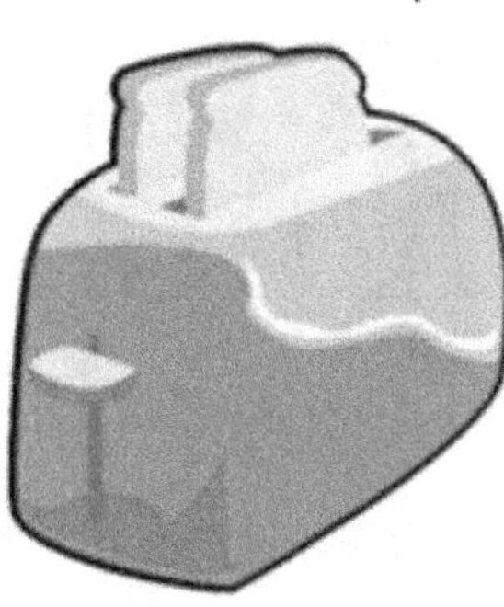

The toaster will toast my bread.

bouilloire

ibrik

The kettle has tea inside.

réfrigérateur

frigorifer

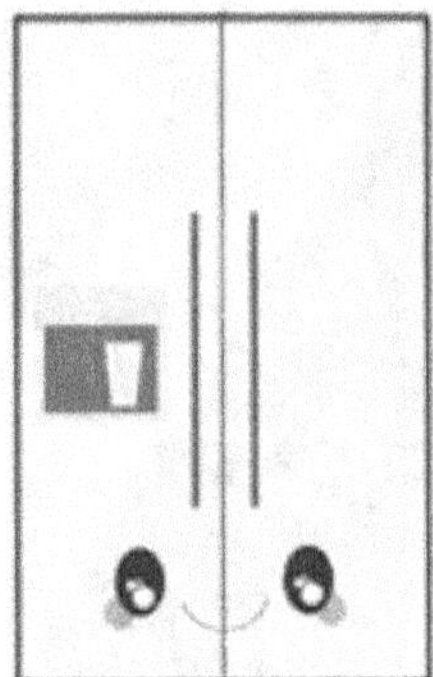

The refrigerator has lots of things inside.

mixeur

blender

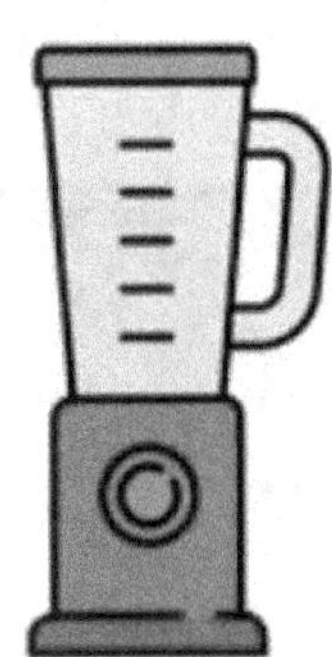

The blender will mix up my fruits.

cabinets

kabinete

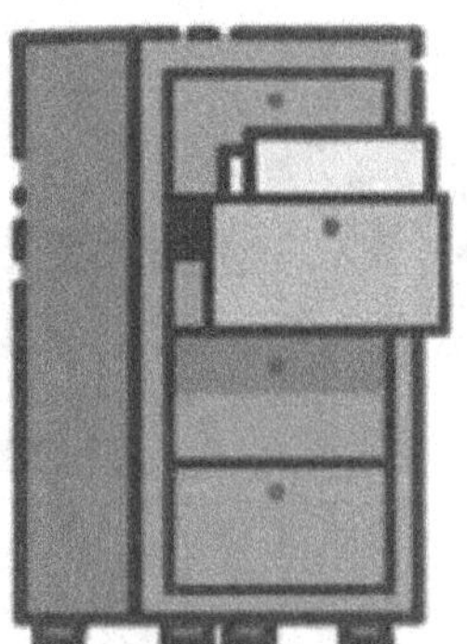

The cabinet has my paper inside.

placard

bufe

The cupboard has lots of books.

four micro onde

microwave

The microwave will heat my food.

arrière

prapa

She has a slender back.

des joues

cheeks

She kisses her mom on the cheek.

poitrine

gjoks

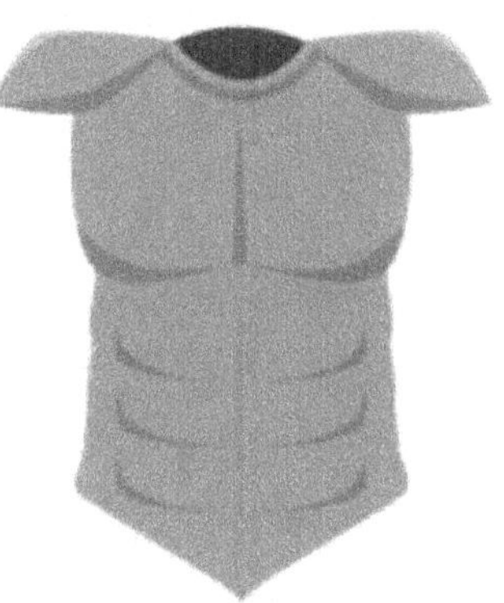

The armor is for your chest.

menton

mjekër

This is my chin!

oreilles

veshët

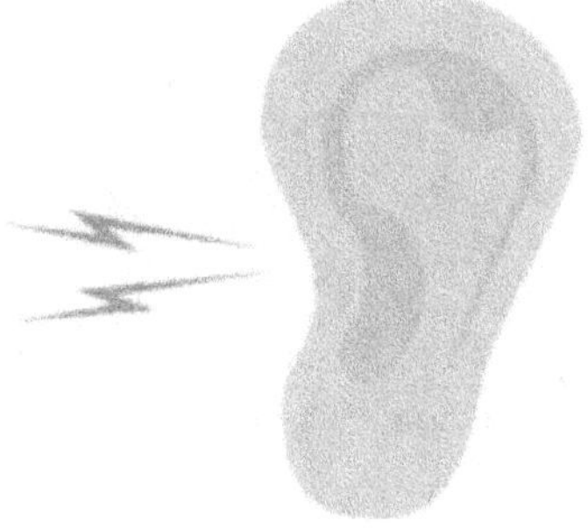

The ear is hearing something.

les sourcils

vetulla

The eyebrows are raised.

yeux

sytë

The eyes are blue.

pieds

këmbët

I have one pair of feet.

des doigts

gishtat

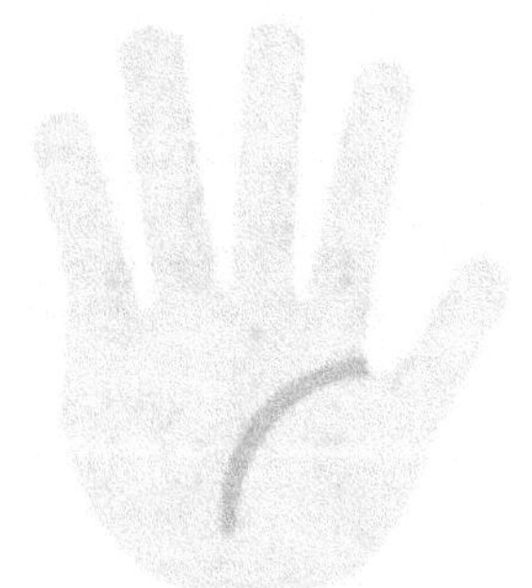

The fingers are waving at us.

pied

këmbë

My foot has five fingers.

front

ballë

My brain is behind my forehead.

cheveux

qime

My hair is long and black.

mains

duart

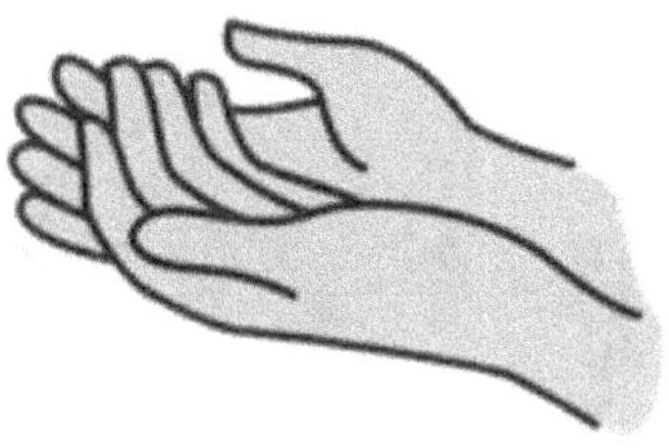

I will wash my hands in the sink.

tête

kokë

She has a big head.

les hanches

hips

The gorilla has his hands on his hips.

les genoux

gjunjë

She is begging on her knees.

jambes

këmbët

The tiger has strong legs.

lèvres

buzët

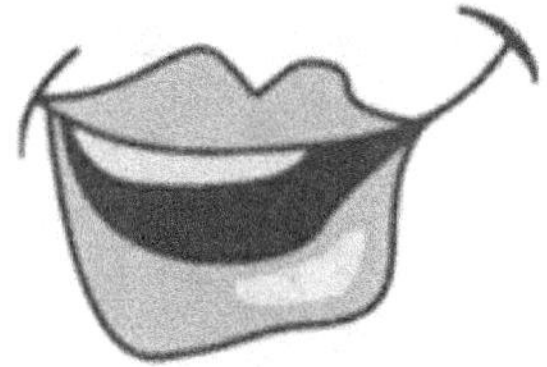

The lips have lipstick on.

bouche

gojë

He is covering his mouth with his hand.

cou

qafë

The necklace is very special to me.

nez

hundë

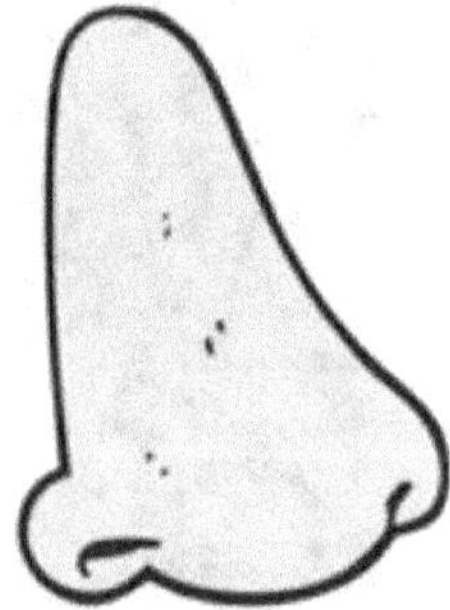

The nose smells something.

épaules

supet

He puts his hands on his shoulders.

estomac

stomak

He has a big stomach.

les dents

dhëmbët

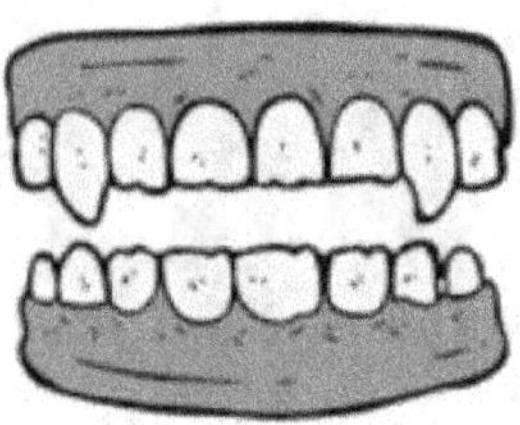

The teeth are clean and white.

gorge

fyt

He has a sore throat today.

les orteils

këpucë me majë

My toes are small.

langue

gjuhë

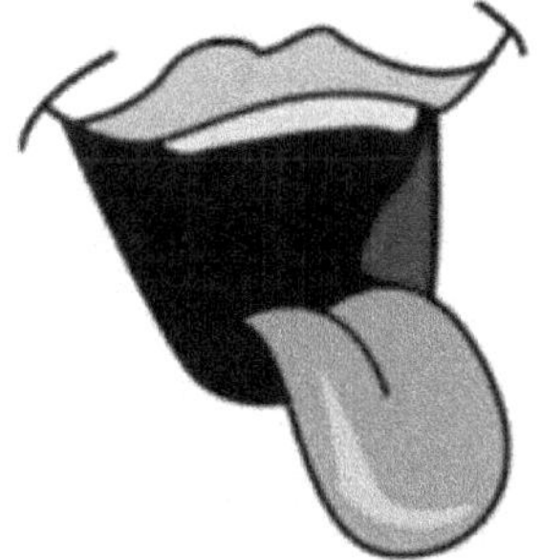

My tongue is licking ice cream.

dent

dhëmb

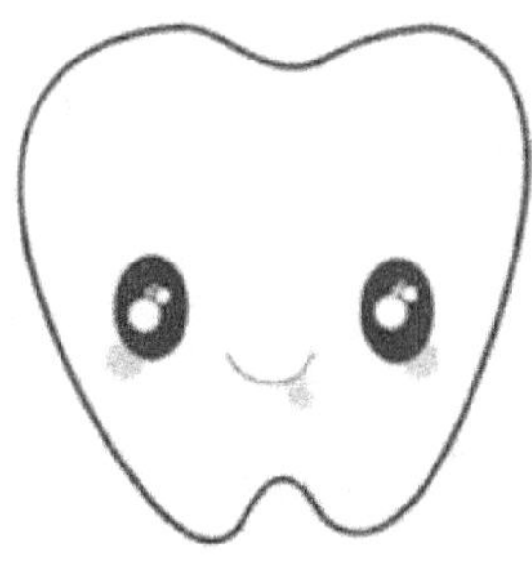

The tooth has big eyes.

taille

bel

He has his hands on his waist.

salopette

pantallona të gjera

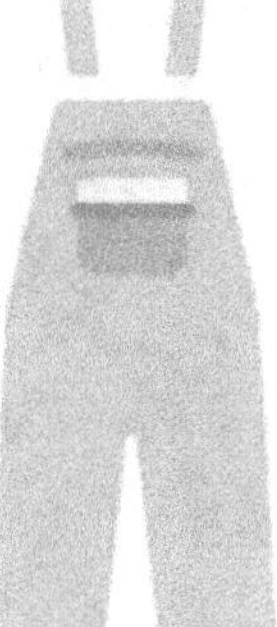

I bought these overalls for you!

mitaines

dorashka

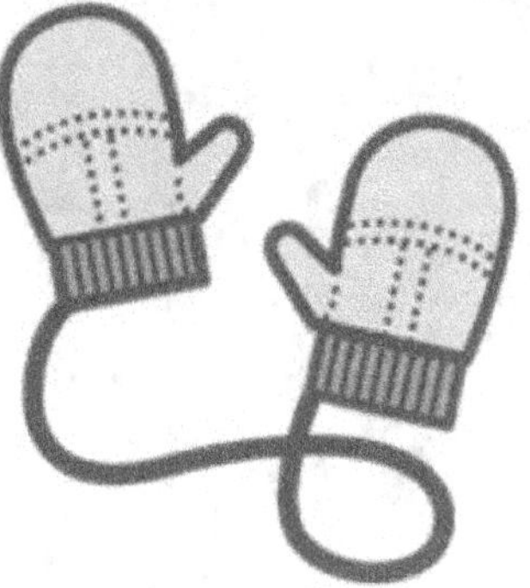

The mittens are very warm.

bonnet

beanie

The beanie is for winter.

tablier

platformë

I wear my apron when I bake.

poupée

kukull

The doll is for my baby sister.

hochets

rraketake

The rattle is for the baby.

jouet

lodër

The toy is very fun.

couche

pelenë

The baby has to wear a diaper.

berceau

lloj djepi

She is sleeping in her bassinet.

bavoir

grykësje

My baby brother has to wear his
bib when he is eating.

octogone

tetëkëndësh

The octagon is saying okay!

triangle

trekëndësh

The triangle has three corners.

carré

katror

Square

The square has four sides.

cercle

rreth

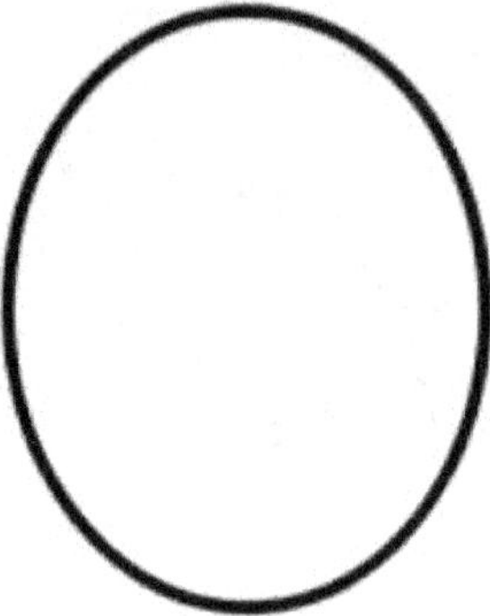

Circle

The circle is round.

ovale

oval

The oval shape looks like a circle.

cœur

zemër

I drew a heart on my paper.

traverser

cross

That sign is a cross.

la flèche

arrow

The arrow is pointing this way.

cube

kub

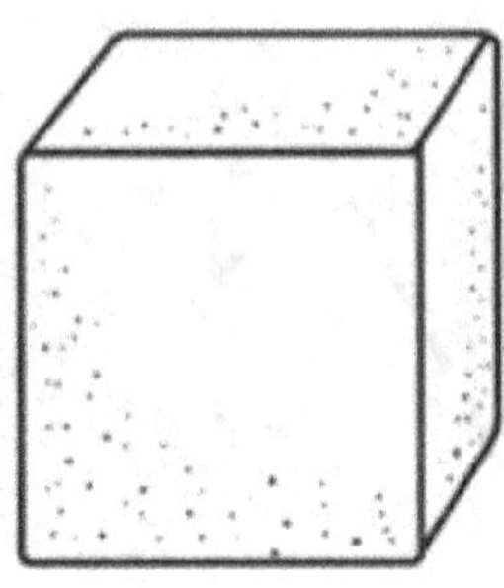

The cube is 3D.

étoile

yll

The star is yellow and shiny.

tir à l'arc

gjuajtje me hark

The archery is where you aim.

badminton

badminton

My favorite sport is badminton.

criquet

kriket

I am very good at cricket.

bowling

klub boulingu

I got one pin down at bowling!

boxe

boks

The boxing gloves are hot.

tennis

tenis

He can hit the ball in tennis.

faire de la planche a roulettes

skateboarding

He skateboards to school.

planche de surf

surfboarding

The shark loves surfing in the ocean.

le hockey

hokej

I like to play Ice hockey.

yoga

yoga

He is closing his eyes and doing yoga.

épée

skermë

They are fencing and dueling together.

aptitude

durim

She will do some fitness in the pool.

gymnastique

gjimnastikë

He can do brilliant gymnastics.

karaté

karate

She is good at kicking in Karate.

volley-ball

volejboll

She is holding a volleyball.

musculation

ngritje peshe

The girl with brown hair can do weightlifting.

basketball

basketboll

He can balance the ball with one finger in basketball.

base-ball

baseball

The little chick is in the finales at baseball.

le rugby

regbi

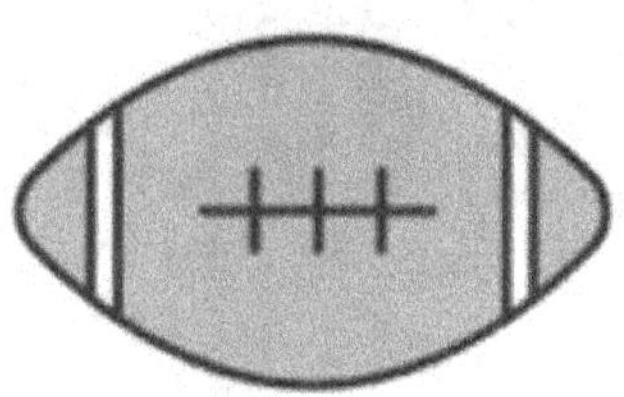

The rugby ball has white stripes.

lutte

mundje

The sumo will compete in wrestling.

course de voitures

gara makinash

He is number one for car racing.

cyclisme

cycling

He is peacefully cycling on the road.

fonctionnement

drejtimin

He is running while listening to his earphones.

tennis de table

pingpongu

My brother and dad will play table tennis.

pêche

peshkimi

He will go to the river to fish.

judo

xhudo

She has a red belt in Judo.

escalade

ngjitje

He will climb the ladder.

tournage

qitje

He is shooting the archery board.

le golf

golf

She is going to compete in the golf competition.

balade

udhëtim

He will ride his scooter.

asseyez-vous

uluni

They are sitting down together.

se lever

ngrihu

She likes to stand up.

bats toi

përleshje

They are fighting over the book.

rire

qesh

He is laughing so hard!

lis

read

She read a picture book.

jouer

luaj

He went to play on the slide.

ecoutez

dëgjoj

He listened for the ice cream cart.

pleurer

qaj

He cried because he got a bad grade.

pense

mendoj

He thought that the test would be hard.

chanter

sing

He sang for the concert.

regarder la télévision

shiko tv

He watched TV the whole night.

danse

valle

She was a good dancer.

allumer

ndez

The light is turned on.

éteindre

fiket

The light is turned off.

gagner

fitore

He won the contest.

mouche

fly

The parrot can fly.

couper

prerje

He was cutting his nails.

désinvolte

hidhni larg

He threw away the garbage.

dormir

gjumë

He slept soundly.

fermer

afër

He closed his mouth shut.

ouvert

hapur

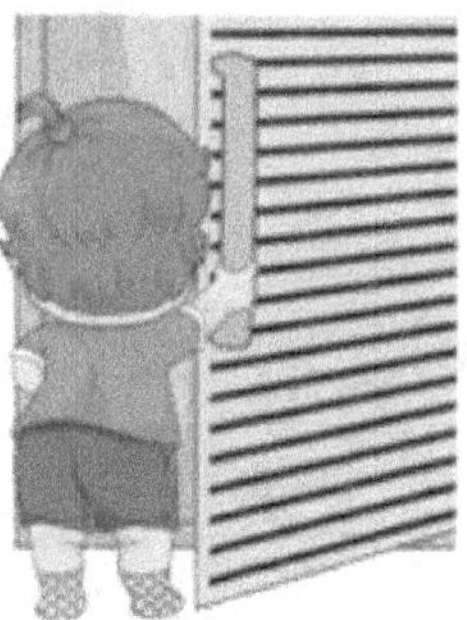

She opened the bathroom door.

écrire

shkruaj

She wrote with a pencil.

donner

jap

Santa gave her a present.

sauter

jump

She had fun jumping.

manger

ha

The shark ate yummy ice cream.

boisson

pije

The old British man drank tea.

cuisinier

kuzhinier

The microwave cooked his soup.

lavage

larje

You need to remember to wash your hands.

attendre

prisni

He was waiting for the bus.

montée

ngjit

She climbed a lot of mountains.

parler

diskutim

Two best friends were talking together.

crawl

zvarritje

The baby crawled on the floor.

rêver

ëndërr

The Sloth dreamed about eating leaves.

creuser

gërmoj

That strong man dug a swimming pool.

taper

duartrokas

The baby clapped her hands.

tricoter

thur

She knits with the purple string.

coudre

qep

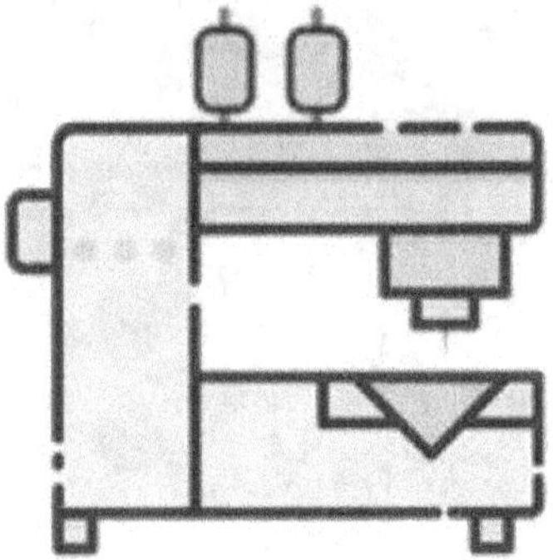

That is a sewing machine.

odeur

erë

The perfume smelled great.

baiser

puthje

He kissed his mother.

étreinte

përqafim

They hugged each other.

ronfler

gërhij

The tiger snored.

baigner

banjë

He took a bath.

s'incliner

përkulur

He bowed to the judge.

peindre

bojë

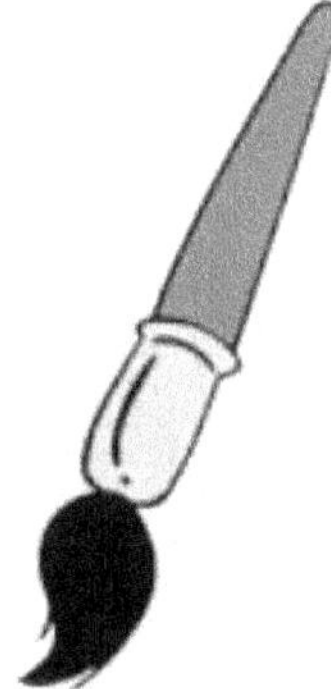

He painted a colorful picture.

se plonger

pikiatë

He dove to the deepest part of the ocean.

ski

ski

The ski was expensive.

empiler

rafte

The books are stacked high.

acheter

blej

They bought cereal.

secouer

shake

They shook hands together.

programmeur

programues

He was a smart computer programmer.

vétérinaire

veteriner

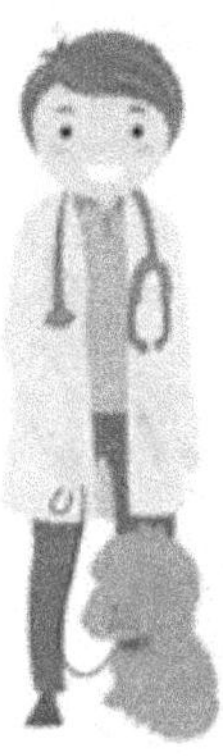

She is a veterinarian.

vendeur de rue

shites rruge

That street vendor sells hot dogs.

mineur

minator

That Miner will find gold.

prof

mësues

The owl is the teacher.

groom

shërbëtor

That Bellboy is fat.

orateur

folës

The chicken is a great Speaker.

boucher

kasap

The Butcher sells fish.

pharmacien

farmacist

That Pharmacist saved a person's life.

réceptionniste

recepsionist

He is a Receptionist.

politicien

politikan

He wants to be a Politician.

guide touristique

udhëzues turne

That Tour guide led us around Japan.

entrepreneur

sipërmarrës

He is an Entrepreneur.

danseuse de ballet

kercimtare baleti

She is training to be a Ballet dancer.

astronaute

astronaut

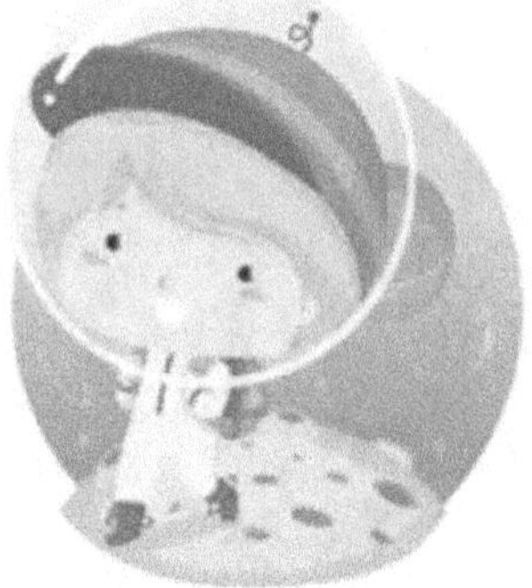

He is a great astronaut.

juge

gjyqtar

That Judge is always fair.

avocat

avokat

The lawyer is serious.

la caissière

arkëtar

She is a cashier at the market.

conducteur de taxi

shofer taksie

He is a fast Taxi driver.

plombier

hidraulik

That Plumber fixes toilets.

musicien

muzikant

She wants to be a Musician like her teacher.

chef

shef

The chef makes fast food.

boulanger

furrtar

That baker is a bread.

artiste

artist

That Artist came from Italy.

acteur

aktor

That actor is famous.

barman

pijeshitës

The Bartender works in a bar.

coiffeur

floktar

That girl is a Hairdresser.

évêques

peshkopët

He is a Bishop.

opticien

syzabërës

She went to an Optician.

fleuriste

luleshitës

She is a great Florist.

écrivain

shkrimtar

He is a famous author.

comptable

llogaritar

My accountant is loyal.

du vin

verë

That wine tastes good.

café

kafe

That coffee is bitter.

limonade

limonadë

The lemonade is refreshing.

chocolat chaud

çokollatë e nxehtë

I drink hot chocolate every day.

milk-shake

milkshake

The milkshake has whipped cream.

eau

ujë

The water is not cold.

thé

çaj

The tea is hot.

lait

qumësht

Milk is white.

bière

birrë

The beer is foamy.

un soda

sodë

The soda is fizzy.

smoothie

gojëmjaltë

The smoothie is a watermelon flavor.

milk-shake

milkshake

The milkshake has whipped cream.

lait de coco

qumesht arre kokosi

The coconut milk is yummy.

du jus d'orange

lëng portokalli

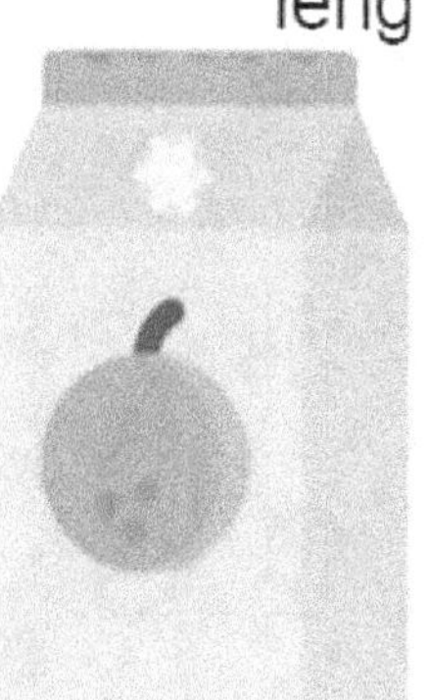

The orange juice is made from oranges.

cacao

kakao

The cocoa is sweet.

fromage

djathë

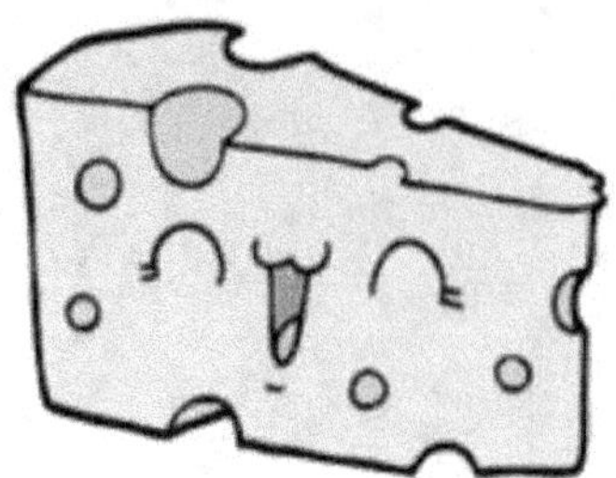

The cheese is creamy.

oeuf

vezë

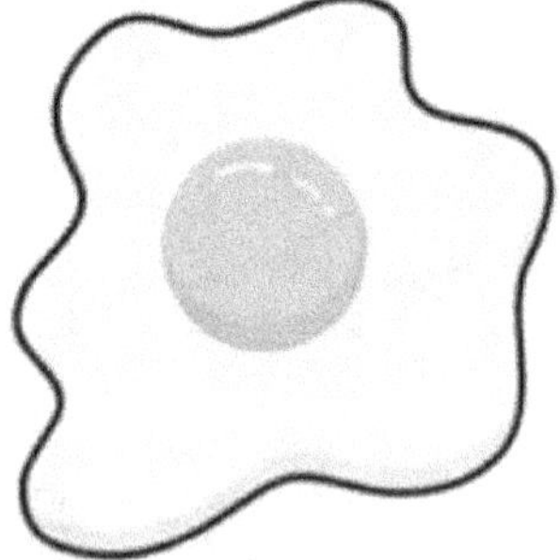

The egg is fried.

beurre

gjalpë

The butter is put on bread.

margarine

margarinë

Margarine looks like butter.

yaourt

kos

That yogurt is popular.

cottage cheese

gjizë

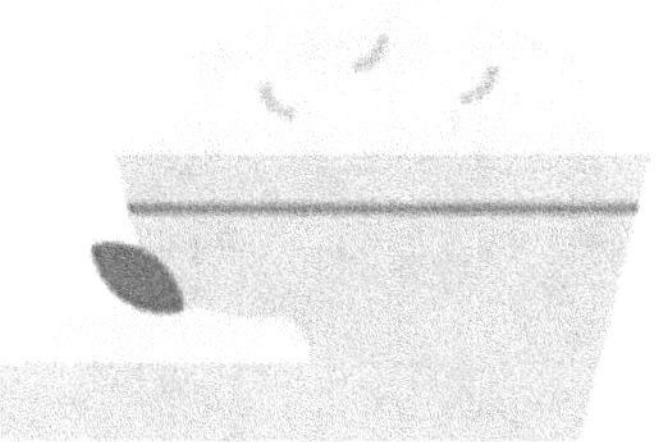

The cottage cheese is put on crackers.

crème glacée

akullore

They have a triple scoop ice cream.

crème

krem

That is a lot of creams.

sandwich

sanduiç

That sandwich is healthy.

saucisse

suxhuk

Americans love sausages.

hamburger

hamburger

That hamburger looks happy.

hot-dog

qen i nxehtë

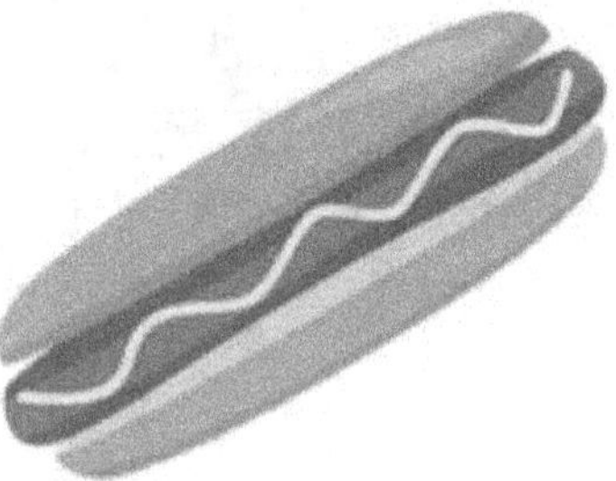

That hot dog has mustard on it.

pain

bukë

That bread is saying hello.

pizza

pica

That pizza is cheesy.

steak

biftek

The steak was grilled.

poulet rôti

pule e pjekur

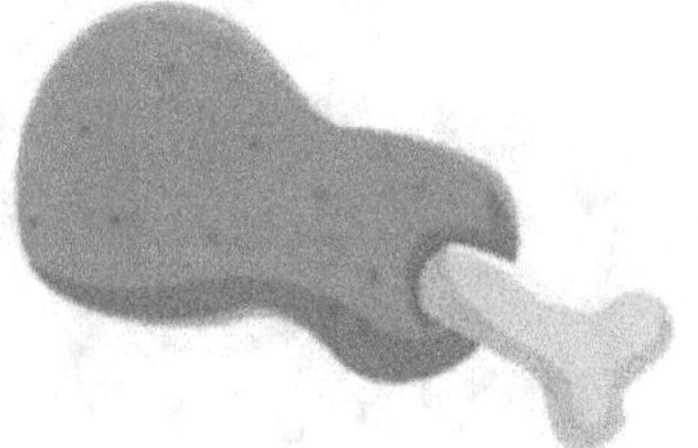

Roast Chicken is delicious.

poisson

peshk

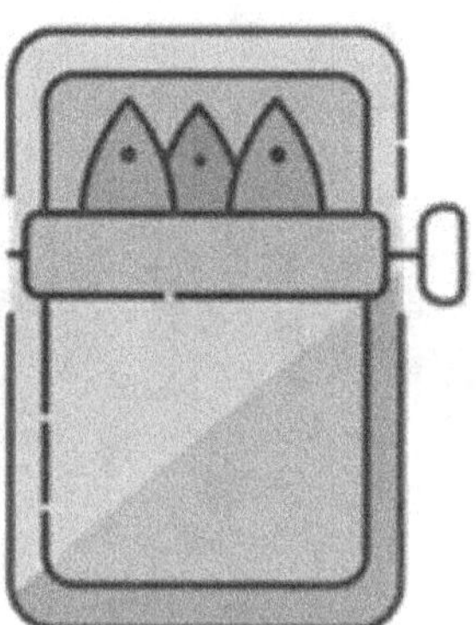

You can buy canned fish in the market.

fruit de mer

ushqim deti

Lobster is expensive seafood.

jambon

proshutë

Ham can be put in sandwiches.

kebab

qebap

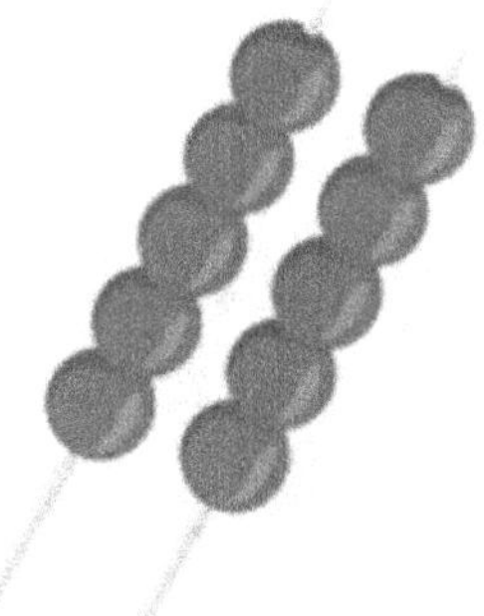

Kebab is a delicacy in America.

bacon

proshutë

That bacon is smiling.

crème fraîche

krem kosi

You can dip your chips in sour cream.

vache

lopë

Cows are black and white.

lapin

lepur

That rabbit is fun to play with.

canard

rosë

That duck is content.

crevette

karkalec

The shrimp has six legs.

porc

derr

That pig is pink and fat.

abeille

bletë

The bee has a stinger.

chèvre

dhi

That goat has a white horn.

crabe

gaforrja

The crab has two big pincers.

cerf

dre

That deer is sleeping.

dinde

turqi

The turkey has a giant tail.

colombe

pëllumb

That dove is carrying a plant.

mouton

dhen

That sheep has fluffy wool.

poisson

peshk

That fish has colorful fins.

poulet

pulë

That chicken is waking everybody up.

cheval

kalë

The horse has a red mane.

chaise

karrige

That wing chair is yellow.

meuble tv

stendë televizive

The TV stand can hold books.

canapé

divan

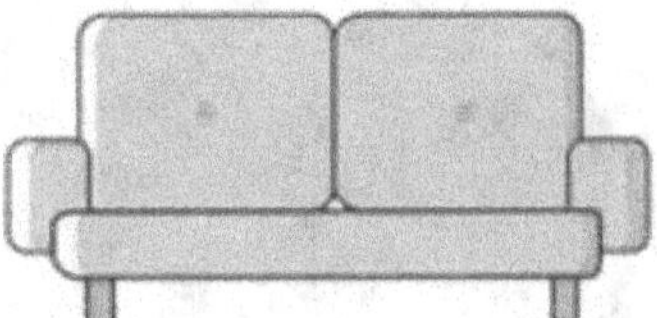

The sofa is comfortable to sit on.

coussins

jastekë

The cushion helps soften your seat.

téléphone

telefon

The telephone is ringing.

télévision

televizion

That television is big.

haut-parleurs

folësit

That speaker is used to increase the volume.

table d'appoint

tryezën anësore

That end table is sparkling clean.

service à thé

set caji

That tea set is from China.

cheminée

fireplace

The fireplace makes me warm.

télécommandes

remotes

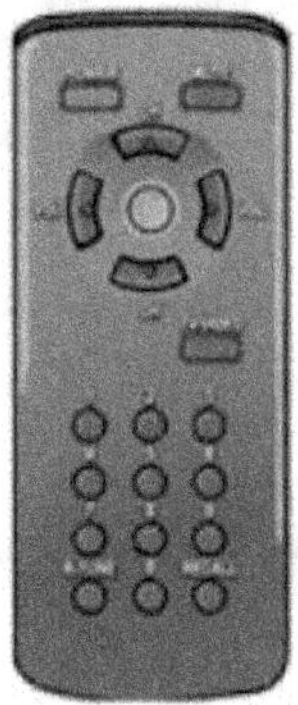

The remote has lots of buttons.

ventilateur électrique

tifoz elektrike

The fan is blowing wind.

lampadaire

drita te dyshemes

The floor lamp is very tall.

tapis

qilim

The carpet is soft and silky.

bureaux

tavolina

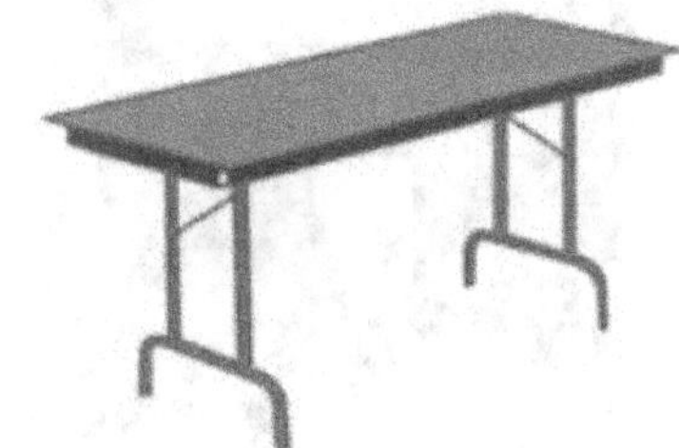

The table is made of wood.

stores

blinds

I will pull the blinds down.

rideaux

perde

She opened the curtains.

image

foto

The picture is about the mountains and the sky.

vase

vazo

The roses are all in a vase.

l'horloge

orë

The alarm clock is beeping.

oreiller

jastëk

The pillow is pink and yellow.

cintre

varëse rrobash

The hat stand has only one hat on it.

mettre la table

tabela e veshjes

I have made up on my dressing table.

lampe de table

llampë tavoline

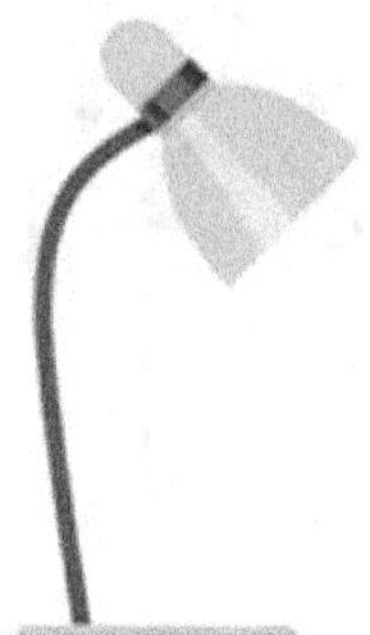

The table lamp will help me see in the dark.

miroir

pasqyrë

The mirror is very tall.

planche a repasser

tavolinë hekurosjeje

Don't touch the ironing board, it's hot!

boîte avec tiroir

kuti me sirtar

You can keep your clothes in the hope chest.

table de chevet

tryezën e shtratit

The nightstand has my lamp on it.

lit

shtrat

The bed is charming.

climatisation

air-conditioner

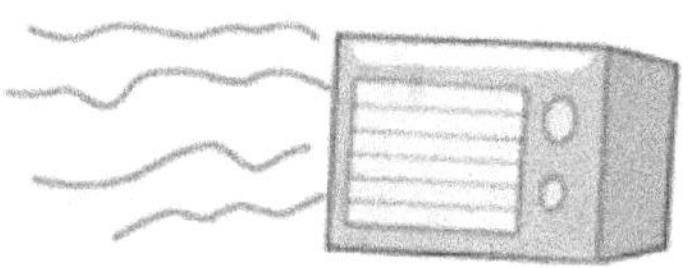

The air conditioner is cold.

cruche

ibrik

The measuring jug has nothing inside.

dentifrice

pastë dhëmbësh

The toothpaste is mint flavored.

brosse à dents

furçë dhëmbësh

The toothbrush has toothpaste on it.

savon

sapun

The soap is very bubbly.

pince à linge

clothespin

The clothespin will clip my clothes.

cintre

hallkë

The hanger is hanging my boots.

sèche-cheveux

tharese flokesh

The hairdryer will blow my hair.

shampooing

shampo

The shampoo is used to clean your hair.

bulle

flluskë

The bubbles are very fun to play in.

brosse

furçë

She is brushing her hair with the brush.

papier toilette

letër tualeti

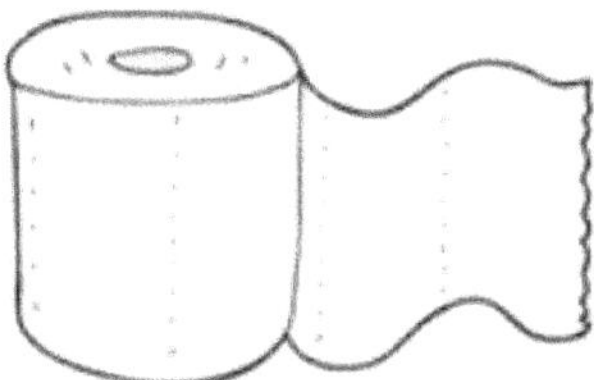

The toilet paper is used to dry your hands.

serviette

peshqir

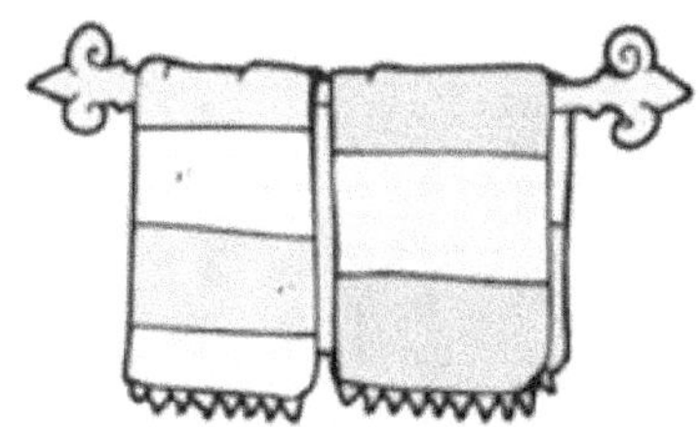

We have two towels on the rack.

corde à linge

tel

My shirt is hanging on the clothesline.

douche

dush

The shower is spraying water.

baignoire

vaskë

The bathtub is comfortable.

lessive

pastrues lavanderi

The laundry detergent is used with the washing machine.

seau

kovë

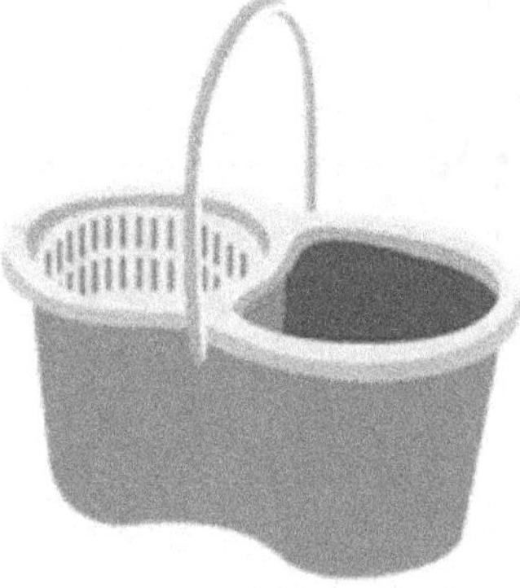

Can you help me fill up the bucket?

vadrouilles

mops

The mop is used for mopping the floor.

savon liquide

sapun i lengshem

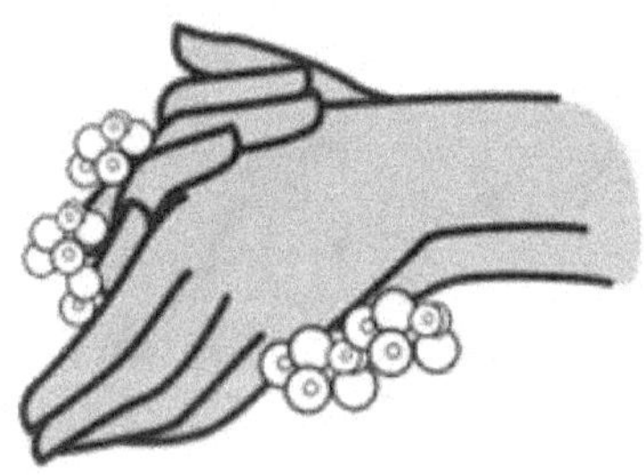

I use soapy water to wash my hands.

lessive en poudre

pluhur larës

I will scoop up the washing powder.

sac poubelle

cante mbeturinash

The trash bag is full of trash.

poubelle

kosh plehrash

You have only to put recylcle trash in the trash can.

les puits

mbytet

You should wash your hands in the sink.

cuvette des toilettes

tas tualeti

She let her bunny use the toilet.

machine à laver

makinë larëse

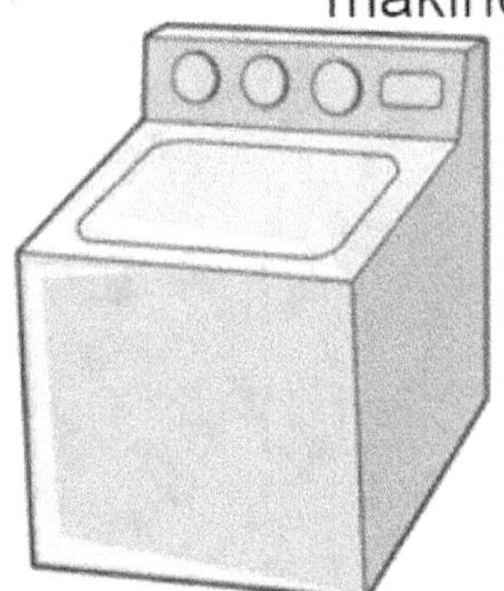

The washing machine wash your clothes.

panier à linge

shporta e rrobave

She is putting all the clothes into the laundry basket.

le rasoir

brisk rroje

He uses the razor to shave his beard.

rasoir électrique

rroje elektrike

The electric razor works faster than the normal one.

crème à raser

krem rroje

The shaving cream is fluffy.

bain de bouche

gargarë

The mouthwash smells very lovely.

coton-tige

syth pambuku

Q-tip can be used for many things.

brosse à cheveux

furça e flokëve

She brushes her hair with her hairbrush.

peigne

krehër

Her dad will comb her hair for her.

nettoyant

cleanser

Put the cap back on the cleanser bottle.

échelle

shkallë

You can measure things on the scale.

papier de soie

letër indi

The tissue is on the counter.

jouets de bain

lodra banjosh

The little duck is a bath toy.

robinet

rubinet

The faucet is broken.

miroir

pasqyrë

He is looking in the mirror.

tapis de bain

qilim banjo

The bath mat is purple and yellow.